HE NATURAL WORK OF ART

e Experience of Romance in Shakespeare's *Winter's Tale*

e LeBaron Russell Briggs Prize
nors Essays in English • 1966

hn Anthony Williams

ARVARD   UNIVERSITY   PRESS

The LeBaron Russell Briggs Prize
Honors Essays in English · 1966

THE NATURAL WORK OF ART
The Experience of Romance in
Shakespeare's *Winter's Tale*

THE NATURAL WORK OF ART

The Experience of Romance in
Shakespeare's *Winter's Tale*

John Anthony Williams

HARVARD UNIVERSITY PRESS

Cambridge, Massachusetts   1967

63965

For Maeve

CONTENTS

THE NATURAL WORK OF ART

The Experience of Romance in Shakespeare's *Winter's Tale*

Shakespearean romance can be defined as a poetic solution to the metaphysical problem, in Elizabethan terms, of the place of Mutability and Nature in human life. It is a means of revising what Sidney called the "trueth of a foolish world" for the purpose of allowing the highest human virtue to appear in its brightest "cullours." "Well may you see *Vlisses* in a storme, and in other hard plights; but they are but exercises of patience and magnanimitie, to make them shine the more in the neere-following prosperitie."[1] We must remember that before turning to the romance form, Shakespeare portrayed in *King Lear* the physical extinction of the powers of virtue at the hands of both accident and planned evil. In that play the experience of suffering is the means by which the chief character is brought to a new understanding of the place of man in nature, and it is by a response to suffering that the audience follows Lear's expanding awareness of life. In *The Winter's Tale* Shakespeare replaces the central experience of pain with that of wonder but still guides his characters to a new level of perception. What they

1

behold at the end of the drama is not a corpse, or a poor, bare, forked animal, but nature's greatest work of art within the human realm—man himself at the center of a beneficent creation, and touched with the grace of a higher order of existence.

Romance, then, involves both a special manipulation of natural law and a peculiar sort of experience in response to the workings of that law. Within the romantic universe certain moral and magical laws are held constant and fully effective[2] for the purpose of subordinating accident and evil to the position of what Sidney called the "wel-wayting hand-mayds of vertue." Specifically, Shakespeare takes the view of Spenser's Nature and her reply to the claims of Mutability.

> All things stedfastness doe hate
> And changed be: yet being rightly wayd
> They are not changed from their first estate;
> But by their change their being doe dilate:
> And turning to themselves at length againe,
> Doe work their own perfection so by fate.
> (VII.vii.58)[3]

Shakespeare could "rightly way" and manipulate events in the tiny state of man by adopting a divine perspective, according to which nature and the arts of man within nature, as well as time and fortune, could be viewed in Christian humanist fashion as "instruments" of beneficent divinity.[4] Nature and time lose their savage potentiali-

2

ties[5] and become the means by which a noble society of men is sustained through the generations.

This sort of control from above, however, is only half the structure of Shakespearean romance. As many critics have emphasized, the playwright was less interested in metaphysical problems *per se* than in their effects on persons and personal relationships.[6] The other half of the romance structure, therefore, is a new mode of characterization. By providing a pre-Christian setting for *The Winter's Tale*,[7] Shakespeare restricts his characters' vision of the divine to the single face of Apollo, whose one temple is on an island separate from the society of the play. He does not, therefore, allow them the certain knowledge of omnipotent divinity operating in everyday affairs that Chaucer, for example, could give to his patiently suffering Custance in *The Man of Law's Tale*. Shakespeare employs for the romance a mode of characterization that stresses the limitations of each character's world view in order to emphasize the fact that the play's pattern of events is beyond any one person's capacity to explain. The only appropriate response is an experience of wonder at the apparently inexplicable. Thus, the characters we follow do not look down on the earth from the throne of Nature but look up at what may often seem a threatening universe. The world of the play presents a series of sharply differentiated views of nature that complement and interact with each other. Each character, by remaining constant to his own status in life, contributes to a pattern of events beyond his level of understanding.

Psychological experience and the ruling power of law become reconciled in Shakespeare's highly original recognition scene at the end of *The Winter's Tale*. The romantic experience of wonder first begets amazement; reason must be humbled so that faith may be awakened. The court of Sicilia becomes profoundly patient as it adjusts its expectations about reality to the visible signs of providence and to the laws that the romance form holds constant. Leontes, by awakening his faith, accepts the "lawfulness" of the final recognition and attains a harmony objectified in the music traditionally associated with the ordered workings of the cosmos as a whole and of every smaller world within it.[8] The meaning of "recognition" that customarily precedes the finale of marriage in earlier Shakespearean comedy is thus greatly increased in significance. We shall begin our discussion of the ways in which *The Winter's Tale* operates according to this scheme of experience and law with an example of the kind of stagecraft needed to further the romance plot.

hearkening back?

This approach assumes that the philosophic and poetic stimulus for the play is only in minor ways to be found in the handful of dramas that can be called romantic tragicomedies of the Elizabethan and early Jacobean stage. One can point to Greene's heroines, especially Fair

4

Margaret of Fressingfield, to the bear and wild man in *Mucedorus,* to the rogues and rustics in *The Maydes Metamorphosis* and *The Thracian Wonder,*[9] to the transformation of statues as well as the festival and satyr dances of masque and antimasque in Jonson and his rivals,[10] and to the 1608 purchase by the King's men of the Blackfriars Theatre, a purchase marking the beginning of a crucial change of dramatic techniques.[11] Finally, one can note parallels in various source materials like Francis Sabie's *The Fissherman's Tale* (1595) and its sequel, *Flora's Fortune,* of the same year.[12] Despite their importance, such sources and conjectured influences on Shakespeare's immediate choice of dramatic characters and incidents fail altogether to explain or even hint at the deeper purposes of his masterly expression.

1. The Stagecraft of Romance

Exit, pursued by a bear is one of the most annotated stage directions in Shakespeare's work. It has been said to mark the point of comic transvaluation of the play,[13] to mingle comic relief with a *frisson* of horror by the use of a disguised acrobat,[14] and to cater to the growing popular taste for bear-play as evidenced by the 1610 elaboration of the similar episode in *Mucedorus.*[15] Wilson Knight comments, "We must take the bear seriously, as suggesting man's insecurity in face of untamed nature."[16] This view of the scene's destructive elements is correct only if we look at untamed nature through the eyes of Antigonus. The business that he is on is "ungentle," as Hermione tells him in his dream vision. To deprive a "bud of nobler race" of the nurturing arts of courtly life and to expose the child to the "savage clamor" of "strange fortune" that may either nurse or destroy it is to remove the babe from all that seems civilized to the royal household. To Leontes the point of the sentence is to consign the alleged bastard to "some remote and desert place, quite out of our dominions" (II.iii.175–176),[17] where he assumes there is no nurturing power to save it. The courtly preconception of the face of nature cannot account for the babe's reception and survival on the shores of Bohemia. We know that Antigonus is mistakenly convinced by his dream of Hermione that she is in fact guilty and the babe a bastard, and in order to accept even this vision in his sceptical or Baconian distrust of the marvelous, he must be "squar'd" by superstition. By following unwittingly, as Hooker might say, the law of his own nature—really, his system of beliefs—and without perceiving the higher power that is making of nature and fortune such "wel-wayting hand-mayds," Antigonus plays his part, as Perdita herself later says when leaving Bohemia, and consigns the blossom to an apparently unfriendly soil.

As the old shepherd enters the scene that appeared so hostile to Antigonus, he brings with him a new concep-

tion of nature and a new level of credulity. If the landscape he crosses suddenly seems less frightening to him
and his son than it did to Antigonus, it is not because,
like Sidney's Arcadians, these rustics compose poetry during their easy hours of watching the flocks, nor because,
like Spenser's Meliboe, they have become sated with the
vanities of courtly life, but because they are simple. As
Polixenes assures Camillo before attending the shepherd's festival, from their "simplicity I think it not uneasy
to get the cause of my son's resort thither" (IV.ii.50–51).
Autolycus preys upon them because they "want but something to be reasonable" (IV.iv.606–607). The shepherd
and his son are what the Elizabethans called "natural,"
that is, mentally incapable of any art. Their conjectures
on the birth of the child record a traditional distrust of
the arts of the court, conceived of as falsely "sophisti-
cated," as Lear says when comparing himself to poor
Tom. "This has been some stair-work," says the shepherd
of *The Winter's Tale*, "some trunk-work, some behind door
work: they were warmer that got this than the poor thing
is here" (III.iii.74–76). We should note that the crafty
courtiers of this description are more like Iachimo or
Oswald than any we see in Sicilia—except, that is, in the
mangled imagination of Leontes.

The shepherd's motives lie in just the sort of superstition that the courtier Antigonus repudiated. "It was
told me I should be rich by the fairies. This is some

changeling: open't . . . This is fairy gold, boy, and 'twill prove so . . . We are lucky, boy; and to be so still requires nothing but secrecy" (III.iii.115–118, 121–124). He at once fits the unusual phenomenon into his scheme of things but with no more adequate an explanation than Antigonus was capable of. The "natural" son's description of the shipwreck and the dinner of Antigonus ("Not where he eats, but where 'a is eaten.") totally neglects in its syntax and enumeration of detail the "mannerly distinguishment" that characterizes the court of Sicilia and that makes so frightening to the mind of Antigonus the sight of "untamed nature." His report is a series of independent clauses, indicating the humorous inability of a mind to structure or subordinate what it sees. The clown has no art either in his speech or his sense of order.

What the scene accomplishes is the transference of the "bud of nobler race" from one realm of value to another, letting it touch for a moment the bare nature that is alien and frightening in one context but merely native in the other. It makes all the difference in the world that Shakespeare had his courtier *exit* rather than *enter, pursued by a bear*, as the 1610 *Mucedorus* requires. By having the bear bout occur offstage, he provides us with an alternate poetic interpretation of the event. It is less important to discuss the bear itself than the ways in which the bear is seen, either as horrific bogey, the antithesis of the civilized gentleman, or as

8

just another dangerous beast in a none too idealized pastoral landscape. The stagecraft of romance, then, advances its plot by opposing different views of nature, which, while never wholly explaining events, gradually introduce us to new levels of experience and more striking "notes of admiration."

2. Madness and the Human Shape of Nature

The most violent storm in *The Winter's Tale* occurs not on the seacoast of Bohemia but in Leontes' mind. It therefore tells us more about the human relationship to nature that it disturbs than does the external threat of beast and raging sea. His fury strains the belief of all who reside in the court precisely because it inverts the essential values of well-tempered civility that sustain Sicilia. At the risk of over-schematization, we will distinguish two conceptions of man's place in nature and his sense of time that are denied by Leontes. The first conception is similar to the idea of the state found in the histories and most clearly represented by the garden scene in *Richard II.* Uncultivated nature grows to wildness because it is fallen; it has succumbed to what Milton called the "ruins of our first parents."[18] The king is the husbandman who must clear away the "briers and darnell of appetite"[19] from his state and his subjects so that virtue and the arts of peace that Burgundy missed in his France may flourish. In the first scene of *The Winter's*

Tale, Camillo describes the state as an organic whole which will be "phisick'd" by the young prince Mamillius. In Sicilia the "fragments" that Coriolanus hated and the Jack Cade rebels, who are most in order when most out of order, are held in their subordinate positions; our attention is focused on the heights of the social scale.

It is Polixenes who clarifies the nature of this royal society by the implicit contrast he draws when recapturing at Hermione's request the idyllic past that he shared with Leontes. "We were, fair queen,/Two lads that thought there was no more behind,/But such a day tomorrow as to-day,/And to be boy eternal . . . We knew not/The doctrine of ill-doing, nor dream'd/That any did" (I.ii.62–65, 69–71). Their youth was characterized not only by innocence but by a relation to time that became impossible after the natural development to manhood. "Temptations have since then been born to's: for/ In those unfledg'd days was my wife a girl;/Your precious self had then not cross'd the eyes/Of my young playfellow" (I.ii.77–80). By growing to maturity the carefree princes took their places in a fallen nature that marks time by the faces of the moon. Polixenes fixes the sublunary position of the court at his first entrance: "Nine changes of the watery star hath been/The shepherd's note since we have left our throne/Without a burden" (I.ii.1–3). The sunny playground of youth has been circumscribed by the walls of a garden, like the one that

Hermione and Polixenes stroll in as Leontes gives vent to his jealous rage (I.ii.180–210). The garden has become the human shape of nature.[20] The world now depends not on innocence and the absence of evil but on mastery of the arts of courtesy and obedience to the sacred laws of society. By courtesy and law, nature and time become the servants of gentility and virtue. In the opening scenes of the play, we sense the milder and highly mannered forms of courtesy and the ease and pleasure with which they are used.

Leontes, as king of such a state, should be most perfectly in control of his rational faculties in order that he may carefully sustain the arts of civility. It is Hermione, however, who best sets the normal tone of courtesy in the first act and it is in her language and conduct that its peculiar grace is best exhibited. Her deft control of conversation reminds us of a mental fencing bout, like the one she refers to while persuading Polixenes to extend his stay. She says to Leontes: "Tell him, you are sure/ All in Bohemia's well . . . he's beat from his best ward" (I.ii.30–33). When Leontes hints of her first success in persuasion, she requests an explanation in imagery of husbandry and the domestication of animals, as well as the sport of kings, horse racing. "Cram's with praise, and make's/As fat as tame things . . . You may ride's /With one soft kiss a thousand furlongs ere/With spur we heat an acre" (I.ii.94–96). And her strategy for detaining Polixenes relies on the distinction in courteous speech between the "limber vows" of ladies, "Your dread 'Verily'" (l. 55), and the more solemn oaths of potent lords. Her whole being, like that of Perdita, seems delicately attuned to the dominant strains of value that sustain the world she inhabits.

The second conception of man's place in nature is subtly stressed in several speeches referring to the succession of generations. When, for example, Camillo hints to Polixenes that he is the bearer of a strange disease, Polixenes requests a clearer statement by summoning up the whole tradition of gentility within which the two men perform their duties. "As you are certainly a gentleman, thereto/Clerk-like experienc'd which no less adorns/Our gentry than our parents' noble names,/In whose success we are gentle,—I beseech you . . ." (I.ii. 391–394). The arts of human education rely for their efficacy on an assured inheritance of the seed of gentility. Time, here, is the instrument of a beneficent nature that regenerates the race of the nobly born. It is because Hermione appears in the court as the highest product of both natural and artificial breeding that she is thought incapable of the crimes Leontes attributes to her. Should the incredible prove true, however, and Hermione be revealed a whore, Antigonus swears that in future he will distrust this regenerating power of nature; he will geld his daughters. "Fourteen [years] they shall not see/To bring false generations" (II.i.147–148). It is Paulina who most clearly affirms the power of "great nature" in the face of Leontes' perversions of reality. With a mocking stress on the legal terminology Leontes has distorted, she says of the new-born Perdita, "This child was prisoner to the womb, and is/By law and process of great nature, thence/Free'd and enfranchised" (II.ii.59–64). This beneficent nature, made wholly effective in the world of romance, is guided in its functions by the unseen hand of divinity, known in the pre-Christian setting of the play as Apollo. It is this face of nature, rather than that of untamed savagery, that points us forward to the second generation and to Perdita, who will embody a sense of nature still richer than anything indicated in the first three acts of the play. Shakespeare's method is to reveal these different values of nature by exposing us to the varying sensibilities of his characters. Our awareness of suprahuman powers develops with theirs; we are denied the overview that sees in the conceptions we have analyzed a single whole. Our best sense of a ruling natural harmony is provided not by Paulina's tirades but by Hermione's patient attuning of expectation to the rhythm of universal change: "There's some ill planet reigns:/I must be patient till the heavens look/With an aspect more favorable" (II.i.105–107). Confident of the values she upholds and the "success" of generations in which she stands, she says quietly at her trial, "For honour,

/'Tis a derivative from me to mine,/And only that I stand for" (III.ii.43–45).

It is within this framework of value—of courtesy, law, and great nature—that the disruptive power of Leontes' madness must be measured. We can readily summarize his distortions of courtesy and law. He interprets the signs of gracious friendship as the art of Acrasia in her Bower of Bliss.[21] He reduces Hermione to an alluring bauble, symbolizing the lustful arts of the enchantress, a medal that Bohemia wears around his neck (I.ii.307–308), and sees her "making practis'd smiles as in a looking glass" (I.ii.116–117). He draws from the imagery of domesticated animals the traditional association with the cuckold's horns: "Come, captain [Mamillius],/We must be neat; not neat, but cleanly, captain:/And yet the steer, the heifer and the calf/Are all called neat . . . Thou want'st a rough pash and the shoots that I have/To be full like me" (I.ii.122–127). Like Adam and Eve in newly fallen Paradise,[22] Leontes here lingers on the obscene meanings implicit in the language Hermione has used for the purposes of gentility. In addition, he distorts at the trial of Hermione the laws of society which he, as king, is meant to uphold, and replaces objective justice with the "rigour" of his own will. He forces Antigonus to swear on his allegiance, the highest bond between lord and vassal, symbolized by the sword which Leontes presents, to commit the "ungentle" act of convey-

14

ing Perdita to an unknown shore. Finally, he replaces art-
ful civilization with an image of the untamed nature it
is meant to refine; he makes of Hermione, the noblest
embodiment of such art, a nameless, languageless mon-
ster.

> O thou thing —
> Which I'll not call a creature of thy place,
> Lest barbarism, making me the precedent,
> Should a like language use to all degrees,
> And mannerly distinguishment leave out
> Between the prince and beggar.

(II.i.82–87)

More significant for the larger plan of the play is the
way in which Leontes, to quote a work much concerned
with the clear perception of nature, leaves "the oracle of
God's works and adores the deceiving and deformed
images which the unequal mirror" of his mind portrays
to him.[23] His image of Perdita as the bastard product
of a lustful union aided by the deceiving arts of cosmetic
decoration is indeed a terrible parody of creation out of
nothing.[24] The ogre that rises brokenly in his mind is
at the opposite extreme of creation from that represented
by nature's most gracious "works"—Perdita and Hermione.
Only at the end of the play will "great nature" present
to his sight a Hermione made glistering by a trial of
patience and endowed with a "better grace" than that
of the human art of the court. The "grace" of courtesy,
so often mentioned in the opening conversations, will

15

be combined with the "grace" of divine providence working through the instrument of nature in the world of man.[25] Thus Hermione, as well as Perdita, will appear like the noble creatures mentioned in *The Book of the Courtier,* who "seem not to have been borne, but rather fashioned with the verie hand of some God."[26] *Castiglione*

The depth to which Leontes sinks in his madness is indicated not only by the way he denies the external creations of nature that sustain nobility through time but also by the way he submits the rule of his soul to "affection," thus making possible things not so held, and "fellowing nothing," as he puts it in his own crazed speech (I.ii. 138–145). As Hooker said concerning the actions of "furious" men, the motive to act "is not in ourselves, but carrieth us, as if the wind should drive a feather in the air, we no whit furthering that whereby we are driven."[27] So says Leontes, driven by his witless affection: "I am a feather to each wind that blows" (II.iii.153). In a sense, he already lies at the mercy of the Fortune to which he thinks he is casting Perdita.[28] In the second half of the play, Florizel will utter a similar line as he declares himself the heir to his affection, the slave of Fortune and fly to every wind that blows. His affection, however, will be directed not toward an ogre created out of nothing, but toward one of the most gracious of creations, Perdita. To summarize Leontes' distortions: he substitutes will for law, jealous imaginings for honorable courtesy, the

16

nothing of his affection for the works of nature, and lastly his own mad sense of truth for divine revelation.

Leontes' rejection of the Oracle of Apollo, the court's highest knowledge of divine intention, can be explained in structural terms, as well as by reference to his madness. At the end of the play, when Hermione has been brought back to life, Paulina says that were such an incredible event merely reported, it would be hooted at like an old tale. We may say that the crazed Leontes can reject the stunning experience of the Oracle that Cleomenes and Dion report precisely because he has not experienced the solemn ceremony and "ear-deaf'ning voice o' th' Oracle" (III.i.9). In order to attune his soul to the music of the cosmos, to attain a "patience" that aligns his expectations with the "process" of great nature, Leontes must himself be reduced to "nothing" in a solemn ceremony, so "something rare" may rush to his knowledge (III.i.20–21). The human shape of nature in the court must come to participate in a deeper vision of nature's works of "art."[29]

3. The Faces of Time

One critic has remarked of Robert Greene that, in his romances, he was Fortune's abject slave and attributed to mere chance and the neutral progression of time all crucial events in his story, including those already supplied with adequate causal explanation.[30] He subtitled *Pan-*

dosto (the major source for *The Winter's Tale*) "The Triumph of Time," thereby indicating his notion of the ruling force of romance. Time, after allowing the harmful effects of Pandosto's (Leontes') jealousy, eventually brings truth to light when, by a chance storm at sea, Dorastus and Fawnia (corresponding to Florizel and Perdita) are brought back to Bohemia with none of the premeditation or providence that Shakespeare supplies.[31] This reliance on Fortune and Time as the chief powers within the natural order also characterizes the romances of Heliodorus, Achilles Tatius, and Longus, the three Greek romancers known to have influenced the Elizabethan writers.[32]

We have already noted the two faces of Time implicit in the first half of Shakespeare's diptych,[33] namely Time as an aspect of fallen sub-lunary nature and Time as the "success" of generations, the instrument of beneficently creating nature. As the events of the play's first generation come to a close, still another Time figure comes forth and tells us with all the authority he can command:

> I that please some, try all: both joy and terror
> Of good and bad, that makes and unfolds error,
> Now take upon me, in the name of Time,
> To use my wings . . . it is in my power
> To o'erthrow law, and in one self born hour
> To plant and o'erwhelm custom.

(IV.i.1–4, 7–9)

18

When Time thus presents himself in his abstract form harking back to the morality plays,[34] he assumes an exaggerated responsibility for the events of the drama, a responsibility such as he possesses in Greene's *Pandosto*. Were we to allow him full credit for the guidance of the play, we should be surrendering to the claim of Mutability before the throne of Spenser's Nature, that her power rules the universe. In fact, Time here functions unwittingly within a higher framework of providence and natural law. All things may be subject to Time within the natural order, but the beneficently guided growth of a royal child cannot be explained solely by reference to so neutral a force. Leontes, royal child though he was, grew out of an idyllic youth into a state of madness. The "grace equal with wondering" (IV.i.24) to which Perdita has grown is the high grace coming by divine providence through the instrument of nature and far beyond the power of the Time figure who confronts us in Act IV, scene 1. He describes his power more accurately when he says he "witnesses" (l. 11) to the changing generations.

His true function here is twofold: first, to convince us that we can accept the sudden acceleration of time, that is, to satisfy our demand for credibility, and second, to align our expectations for the future with Time's rhythm, which is also, of course, that of nature and providence.

19

The second is really the obverse of the first, but their intimate association is a brilliant linking of technical necessity with the profoundest purposes of the play. When Time says, "Impute it not a crime/To me . . . that I slide/O'er sixteen years," (ll. 4–6) and asks that "your patience" allow this, he requests our compliance not only with a dramatic convention, as does the chorus in *Henry V*, but also with the divine law whose unwitting "servitor," as Hooker would say, Time is. We submit to the beneficent order of nature just as do Time himself and the characters of the drama. The chorus is a way, therefore, of drawing us into the conditions of experience that the protagonists share.

Hooker provides a brief definition that throws light on the significance of "patient" adjustment to "law" for the Renaissance mind. "Law . . . is a directive rule unto goodness of operation."[35] Law is really the rule by which a being attains its teleological end, or good; following law is, in Spenser's phrase, a working toward perfection, or mode of existence best suited to a particular being—the end for which it was created and fitted by God into the universal order. The word "law" carried a moral meaning, as did the word "art," that it now lacks. In a play full of parallels and oppositions, no more important parallel can be found than the one that links Time's request of "patience" from the audience to Paulina's request of the same quality from Leontes before the awakening of Hermione's "statue." Leontes must not only accept the passage of sixteen years and receive Hermione in the state to which Time has brought her, he must also agree that what Paulina reveals is "lawful." "Those that think it is unlawful business/I am about, let them depart" (V.iii. 96–97). Like Leontes in the final scene, the audience is asked to awaken its faith in the ability of law and providence to transcend human expectation and to insure by their natural working a restoration of life. With this heightened sense of Time and law we are in a better position to respond to the richest sense of nature yet encountered in the play, that embodied in Perdita.

4. Versions of Pastoral

Act IV of *The Winter's Tale* contrasts five versions of pastoral nature, each of which is revealed in the speech of a different character—Perdita, Florizel, the old shepherd, Autolycus, and Polixenes. The stagecraft of the act shows very clearly that these different views complement each other in action even when they oppose each other in speech. No character can fully comprehend the course of the play's action; unconsciously, however, all work toward a common end as though their different "natures" were indeed but separate aspects of a greater whole. Throughout the festival scene it is Perdita who provides the touchstone by which the other views of nature are measured.

Our first poetic "view" of Perdita is through the eyes of Florizel, the disguised prince, the royal and "gracious mark o' th' land." His love for her lends to his speech a quality of metaphor that most clearly echoes the disguised heroes of Sidney's *Arcadia*.[36] He exalts his love to the rank of a goddess—Flora, "peering in April's front." He transforms the sheep-shearing into a meeting of the gods and recalls that "Golden Apollo" himself became a "poor humble swain as I seem now" (IV.iv.30–31)[37] for the sake of a love far less chaste than his own. He ranks the power of his love above Fortune, above the courtly order in which he has so high a place, and, if need be, above reason itself.

Although Perdita accepts her "unusual weeds" in the holiday humor of the festival, she is so finely attuned to natural differences of degree that she continually modulates the poetry of Florizel's imagination and draws it away from the realm of literary pastoral in which it dwells. She measures time not by the "watery star" that Polixenes mentioned in Act I but by the bright sun of the diurnal order that shines on all alike (446–447). The same sun reveals the obvious difference in rank between the lovers that "forges dread" to her mind. "Your high self . . . you have obscured with a swain's wearing and me, poor lowly maid,/[am] Most goddess-like prank'd up" (7–10). Just as Perdita withdraws herself from full participation in Florizel's poetic garden, so the speech of her foster father distinguishes her still more clearly from the simple and earthy rustics among whom she has lived. "When my old wife lived, upon/This day she . . . welcom'd all, serv'd all;/Would sing her song and dance her turn; now here/At upper end o' th' table, now i' th' middle;/On his shoulder, and his; her face o' fire with labour" (55–61). Perdita is not the carousing wife of this vivid speech. "You are retir'd,/As if you were a feasted one, and not/The hostess of the meeting" (62–64). Though she is not the hostess of rustic tradition, she is, as Camillo says, a mistress to most that teach, even though she lacks instructions (583–584). As both Florizel and the old shepherd, though in more homely fashion, assert, "All [her] acts are queens" (146). The peculiar grace that she exhibits as hostess to Polixenes cannot be accounted for either by courtly nurture, literary goddesses, or rustic manners. Her flower speeches eloquently differentiate the level of nature she knows from that of literary pastoral, a mythological eternal garden, or a human garden of courtly cultivation.

In her "debate" with Polixenes, Perdita reveals a sensitivity to nature as the sufficient tutor and cultivator of life. She has had no other instruction than that of the noble seed planted within her. Her foster father, most unlike the patient Meliboe, is capable of referring to the period of nurture itself as a simple nuisance: "I would there were no age between ten and three-and-twenty, or

that youth would sleep out the rest" (III.iii.59–60). She
has found "art" unnecessary in any of Puttenham's four
senses of "coadiutor," "mender," "imitator," or "contrary"
of nature. Perdita thinks of art only in the sense of
"streaking" or "painting" natural beauty for lustful purposes. She thus rejects the "streak'd gillyvors": "I'll not
put/The dibble in earth to set one slip of them;/No
more than, were I painted, I would wish/This youth
should say 'twere well, and only therefore/Desire to
breed by me" (99–103). When Polixenes replies to her,
he speaks from the wholly different conception of nature
that is associated with the court. Only careful human
cultivation ensures perfect growth, though without the
original noble seed all human efforts would be vain.
"This is an art/Which does mend nature—change it
rather—but/The art itself is nature" (95–97). It is ap-
parent that Polixenes' conception of nature does not include the idea of an unnurtured princess—like Perdita—
and that Perdita's view of art does not include, at least
in horticultural matters, the idea of beneficial human
tampering. Neither view is wrong; pure nobility of Nature
and the grace of Art will eventually merge in the statue
of Hermione. And during the action of the festival scene
itself, Camillo, a courtly husbandman, will help guide
the love of Perdita and Florizel.[38]

More important than this brief "debate" for understanding Perdita's relation to nature are the contrasts implied in her own poetry between her and other pastoral figures. When she presents flowers to Camillo and Polixenes, she reveals a sensitivity to the life of each plant within the seasonal cycle. "Sir, the year growing ancient, /Not yet on summer's death, nor on the birth/Of trembling winter, the fairest flowers o' th' season/Are our carnations and streak'd gillyvors" (79–82). When presenting her gift, appropriate "to men of middle age" (108), she mentions not only the fact that the flowers belong to middle summer, but that one of them, the marigold, "goes to bed wi' th' sun/And with him rises weeping" (105–106). Her imagery tries to harmonize the cycles of the day, of the seasons, and of the ages of man. When turning to the young maidens, she wishes for "flowers o' th' spring, that might become your time of day" (113–114). She recalls the daffodils "that come before the swallow dares, and take/The winds of March with beauty" (119–120), the primroses "that die unmarried, ere they can behold/Bright Phoebus in his strength" (123–124).

Such imagery of frail beauty and amorous dalliance (daffodils taking the winds of March with beauty) brings to mind Edenic and mythological pastoral like that in Spenser's Garden of Adonis or the flower and Eden passages in later poems like "Lycidas" and Book IV of *Para-*

dise Lost. Those unfallen pastoral worlds, however, are sharply distinguished from Perdita"s "rustic garden" in two ways.

First, Perdita, unlike the poet of "Lycidas" who can command all the flowers and other pastoral forces needed to memorialize his "sad occasion dear"[39]—or for that matter, unlike Flora in Peele's *Arraignment of Paris*—cannot reach through time to pluck the flowers of spring: "O, these I lack,/To make you garlands of" (127–128). Yet she does not regard Time as an enemy, as did Spenser in his Garden of Adonis where Time the destroyer "with his scyth addrest,/Does mow the flowring herbes and goodly things" (III.vi.39). For Perdita Time is expressed in the seasonal cycle; it appears only as an instrument of fruitful growth and blossoming, not of destruction. In a sense, then, she comes close to the view of Spenser's Nature replying to Mutability that all things change, but by their change "their being doe dilate."

Second, Perdita's relation to nature is not the fragile one of seemingly innocent and eternal youth such as Polixenes recalled in Act I. Every Edenic garden existing before the division of time into seasons and the fall of man is indeed frail and vulnerable to a loss of innocence; the typical figure of such an unfallen state is Proserpina, whom Perdita refers to at lines 116–117. Shakespeare's heroine cannot be "frighted" like the daughter of Ceres and "let fall" the flowers of innocence. The time of the scene is put at late summer in order to emphasize the contrast between mature blossoming associated with that period and the frailer beauties of new-budding spring. We see Perdita not as a bashful virgin but as one eager to embrace Florizel, "not like a corpse; or if—not to be buried,/But quick, and in mine arms" (131–132). Like Spenser's Britomart, she embodies a vigorous and dynamic chastity.[40] The sense of growth that her person embodies and that her poetry so effectively controls is summarized in her famous image of the shepherdesses "that wear upon your virgin branches yet/Your maiden-heads growing" (115–116). Fertility is unmistakably associated in the image with blossoming; loss of maidenhead no longer seems a negative conception, as it was in the case of Proserpina, but an attainment of mature beauty. The courtly equivalent of this branching image was less successful in controlling the implications of growth: "There rooted betwixt them then such an affection which cannot choose but branch now" (I.i.23–24). Camillo's sentence seems ominous in retrospect because its use of "branch" (both "to grow" and "to divide") and of "affec-tion" (both "friendly love" and "fancy" or mad "passion") is ambiguous. In Leontes' mind affection turns to mad-ness and "fellows" nothing. Perdita's nature imagery avoids the hint of artificiality in courtly speech because it is used instinctively through close acquaintance with the floral life it describes. In courtly language such imagery is a mark of wit and human poetic art. Perdita's sensibility and its poetic expression are a natural art that selects from the rustic landscape the flowers that have nothing to do with either the court, sheep-raising, or the roguery of Autolycus.

By adding to his pastoral landscape this last figure, the cut-purse Nip and pick-pocket Foist of Greene's *Second Conny-Catching* (1592),[41] Shakespeare provides yet another version of nature that inspires its own kind of poetry.

> The white sheet bleaching on the hedge,
> With hey! the sweet birds, O how they sing!
> Doth set my pugging tooth an edge;
> For a quart of ale is a dish for a king.
>
> The lark, that tirra-lirra chants,
> With heigh! with heigh! the thrush and the jay,
> Are summer songs for me and my aunts,
> While we lie tumbling in the hay.
>
> (IV.iii.5–12)

Autolycus, with his "pugging" or "thieving" tooth, brings into view the sheets that are his prey and the doxies and "aunts" that are his whores in the midst of the singing birds and summer flowers of the rustic scene. His bawdy comic genius is at the opposite extreme from Perdita's sturdy innocence, yet he too is finally subordinated to the larger plan of the play. We will consider him briefly first as a dramatic contrast to Perdita and secondly as another instrument furthering the romance plot.

Autolycus enters the festival scene as a zany Orpheus, dangling the bright rags and alluring baubles ("Masks for faces and for noses:/Bugle-bracelet, necklace amber") that are the tools of disguise and cosmetic art. In the context of the court, these trinkets represent a deceiving art and thus appear to a crazed Leontes as the images of a lustful union. To Perdita they appear as the devices of a painted whore. For the rustics, however, no sin is involved; because they are "natural" they enjoy such holiday decoration in a world otherwise devoid of any art. Their attraction for Autolycus' "scurrilous" tunes and his baubles helps to differentiate them further from the natural princess who lives among them. In fact, it is rustic artlessness, the simplicity of shepherds who "want but something" to be reasonable men (606), that gives Autolycus success in his rogue's art. By his ballad trumpery, he is able to lull his "natural" listeners into a state of "nothing" that is a parody of the state to which Cleomenes and Dion were reduced before the Oracle of Apollo. "No hearing, no feeling but my sir's song, and admiring the nothing of it" (613–614). He becomes a thieving husbandman as he tames his "herd" (609), and gathers a harvest of purses: "So that in this time of lethargy, I picked and cut most of their purses" (615–616).

Whereas Perdita is always aware of her disguise as a pretense to a rank she does not deserve, Autolycus flourishes by his manipulation of garments. A shedding of clothes has none of the significance for him that it does for a

Lear or an Antony; his station in life changes with his costume. He becomes a courtier cap-a-pie by donning Florizel's apparel and pocketing his "beggar's excrement." He depends for success in his art on what the "conniving" of the gods brings his way; Fortune is his guiding deity in a way it could never be for Perdita, who knows that "affliction cannot take in the mind," and whose soul requires only its innate noble seed—not an enterprising and deceiving art—in order to flourish.

After the rogue has reported the success of his art in taming the rustics, Camillo comes forward from his conference with Florizel and Perdita and says: "Who have we here? We'll make an instrument of this; omit/Nothing may give us aid" (625–627). By removing the changeable garments that symbolize Autolycus' humorous vice, the counselor Camillo, ghost of the Mercy figure in the moralities, transforms him into the unwitting tool of his greater plan to convey the lovers to Sicilia. Yet Autolycus, simply by remaining constant to his profession, furthers still more significantly not only the return of Perdita but also the discovery of her identity when he thwarts the shepherd's visit to Polixenes and shuffles him aboard the ship bound for Sicilia. As he says in the last speech of Act IV, "If I had a mind to be honest, I see Fortune would not suffer me: she drops booties in my mouth." Without understanding the ultimate significance of this bit of knavery, Autolycus plays his part, as Perdita says when donning her disguise (655–656), and helps bring about the final discovery.

This section of the play best illustrates the ways in which all characters, speaking from widely different points of view, continually complement each other in thought and action, and refine by means of the arts at their disposal one part of a larger pattern of events. Not only does the thieving husbandry of Autolycus further the action; the courtly husbandry of Camillo also comes into play. After Polixenes' furious dispersal of the festival, Florizel's only plan of action is to submit himself to Fortune and make himself heir to his affection instead of heir to the throne. "We profess/Ourselves to be the slaves of chance, and flies/Of every wind that blows" (540-542). The lovers fail to provide an adequate means of control over their own course of action. Camillo's reasonable art guides the powerful force of a chaste yet dynamic love. He recommends a plan much wiser than what he calls "a wild dedication of yourselves/To unpath'd waters, undream'd shores; most certain to miseries enough" (567–569). His view of nature is like that of Antigonus; beyond the sway of courtly art he can see no beneficent power, only the rule of indifferent Fortune. He himself, though guiding the effects of both the art of Autolycus and the love of Perdita and Florizel, acts without any higher knowledge. He tells us explicitly that his plan for Florizel will serve a deep motive of his own. "Now were I happy, if/His going I could frame to serve my turn,/Save him from danger . . . [and]/Purchase the sight again of dear Sicilia" (509–512). We further sense the inadequacy of his world view when he utters what may be called a Shakespearean heresy in the line, "Prosperity's the very bond of love." Perdita at once corrects him. "I think affliction may subdue the cheek,/But not take in the mind" (577–578). This minor exchange is typical of the ways each view of nature presented in the play complements the others.

The stagecraft of romance seems, at this point, to focus our attention most clearly on the invisible power that is somehow making "instruments" of every character and every action. Although the five versions of pastoral nature detected in the fourth act begin by impressing us with their peculiar vitality, they all end by being merged and working toward a common end, though without being able to explain more than a fraction of the total pattern. In a way, the scene on the seacoast of Bohemia is emblematic of the rhythm throughout the play. We are always approaching the limits of explanation and of the efficacy of one realm of value; ultimately we can only be "patient" in the sense of aligning our expectation to that of the play's ruling natural law. We can say of Nature in *The Winter's Tale*, as Milton did of Truth, that it is not impossible she may have more shapes than one. It is the purpose of the play's last act to reveal what unity the natural perspective of man may attain.

5. Modes of Belief and Recognition

When Dorcas and Mopsa ask of Autolycus' fantastic balladry, "Is't true, think you?" they pose unwittingly one of the central questions of Shakespearean romance, the question of credibility. In response to an authentic old wives' tale, like the one Mamillius begins to tell about an old man who lived by a churchyard, or the one in Peele's play about "a king or a duke or a lord," the appropriate level of credibility is best summed up by the prototypical old wife herself, "Either hear my tale or kiss my tail." Belief is deliberately strained because fantasy is part of the story's power to entertain. For Dorcas and Mopsa, it is almost believable that an extravagant poetic justice should prevail, that a usurer's wife should give birth to money bags and that a "cold fish" should be physically transformed into the inhuman shape her soul has assumed. The tale is able to shift human appearance into whatever kind of body its inner spirit makes appropriate. Wish projection has its Platonic side, and full consent to such storytelling requires a suspension of critical inquisitiveness.

At first glance, the fifth act of *The Winter's Tale* seems to demand a similar mode of belief. Amazed courtiers report, "The Oracle is fulfilled; the king's daughter is found: such a deal of wonder is broken out within this hour that ballad-makers will not be able to express it . . . This news . . . is so like an old wives' tale that the verity of it is in strong suspicion" (V.ii.22–28). The report of

33

Antigonus' death is "like an old tale still, which will have matter to rehearse, though credit be asleep and not an ear open" (V.ii.62–64).

Romance, in the phrase Yeats used of tragedy, is being wrought to its uttermost. The mode of belief required by the ultimate experience of romantic wonder is not a suspension of inquiry but, as Paulina says to Leontes in the last scene, an "awakening of faith." In order to accept the phenomenon of the statue, those who look upon it must broaden their conception of reality, of the relation between nature and art. Rather than a miracle of revealed religion, however, the court of Leontes must accept a wonderful product of several kinds of art and nature. The conception suggested by the scene of the statue's transformation is summarized in a statement by Sir Thomas Browne. "Nature is not at variance with Art, nor Art with Nature, they both being servants of [God's] providence . . . In brief, all things are artificiall; for Nature is the Art of God."[42] "Art" must be taken in the broadest sense as any kind of fashioning and molding for some purpose. We might say that the debate between Perdita and Polixenes in Act IV is here resolved by showing that the concepts of "Art" and "Nature" are not mutually exclusive, but always work together.

The statue is first presented as the work of the mimetic sculptor Julio Romano, whom the courtiers pronounce the perfect ape of nature. His art can capture both the inward and "outward fair," as did the representation of Philoclea in Kalendar's garden house.[43] "He so near to Hermione hath done Hermione, that they say one would speak to her and stand in hope of answer" (V.ii.99–101). This form of art wages a sort of friendly rivalry with nature.[44] The second level of art is that of courtly nurture and human moral training; it was clear at Hermione's entrance that she was already the gracious embodiment of refined civility. We have also referred to the still higher "art" that is crucial to the maintenance of noble stock through successive generations—the "art" of nature that captures the perfect copy of the noble parent. Paulina establishes the analogy between the imitative painter and great nature when she prays that the mind of the new-born Perdita may have "'mongst all colours /No yellow in't, lest she suspect, as he does,/Her children not her husband's!" (II.iii.105–107). When Leontes greets Florizel, he too stresses this high art that recreates the noblest men: "Your father's image is so hit in you,/ His very air, that I should call you brother . . ." (V.i. 126–127).

Still above this third art is that which Hermione unconsciously hinted at during her trial when she said that a "better grace" would be the result of her patient suffering. It is "grace" in the sense of providential care in the natural realm. We might say that this art is in fact the art of romance, for it is providence that makes of all the instruments in the natural realm and all the levels of human society, from the rogue to the courtier, the servants and "wel-wayting hand-mayds" of nature's greatest artifact. It is this fourth art that lends to Hermione's "statue" an added brilliance, making her appear, as expressed in *The Book of the Courtier,* like one that seems "not to have been borne, but rather fashioned with the verie hand of some God."[45] Hermione appears as a work of art in order that the suprahuman elements in her "fashioning" may be clearly stressed.

"But yet, Paulina, Hermione was not so much wrinkled, nothing/So aged as this seems" (V.iii.27–29). Just as Perdita's poetry emphasized time as a progression toward blossoming maturity, so the "carver's excellence" clearly portrays the passage of sixteen years. The "patience" Paulina demands of Leontes is a perception of the beneficent face of time; aging is no longer seen as decay but as progress toward a new glistering humanity. "Does not the stone rebuke me/For being more stone than it?" (V.iii.37–38). We recall that Ariel, the spirit of Prospero's art, reminded his master of the need for human pity; here the "arts" of the statue provide Leontes with a reminder of the same sort. When Leontes asks the crucial question, "What was he that did make it?" he unconsciously draws our attention to the higher art of nature herself. "Would you not deem it breath'd? And that those veins/Did verily bear blood?" (V.iii.64–65).

Leontes "recognition" is a deeper reverence for the effects of law and time.

Pericles, after his long sufferings, attained a harmonious relationship with the universal order that was symbolized by his hearing the music of the spheres. Paulina's function in the "statue" scene is to prolong Leontes' experience of wonder until he reaches a state in which the "madness" caused by the statue becomes a "cordial comfort" (V.iii.77) to him. He is brought to a condition opposite to that of his earlier madness during which he said to Camillo that the poisoning of Polixenes would be "cordial" (I.ii.318), that is, "reviving" to his heart. What inspired that madness was the monstrous product of his inner imagination. The pleasing lunacy that afflicts him in the "statue" scene is inspired by a natural work of art that gathers to itself all the graces of courtesy or human cultivation, of mimetic artistry, of nature's noble "buds," and of providential care itself. All the laws of the romantic universe have worked together to produce the "statue." The music that accompanies its descent symbolizes, as in the case of Pericles, the attainment of a harmony with the universal order that has brought human life to this height of beauty and artistry. Leontes is not merely falling in love again with his long lost wife. He is becoming "enamoured" of all the qualities of art that are united in Hermione.

"It is requir'd/You do awake your faith . . . Those

that think this is unlawful business/I am about, let them depart . . . Music, awake her; strike!/'Tis time; descend . . . Strike all that look upon with marvel" (V.iii.94–96, 98–100). With these words Paulina brings into the society of Leontes' court the solemn ceremony and sense of submission to natural as well as man-made law that heretofore were associated with the Isle of Delphos. By replacing the theophany of *Pericles* and *Cymbeline* with a recognition wholly restricted to the human realm, Shakespeare gathered the power of his art to a human focus unmatched in the other late plays. The experience of wonder that his romance attains is the point at which the many views of nature that we have analyzed begin to merge; patience, or attunement to the harmony of the natural order, becomes the condition for a unified vision of that order. While controlling the laws of his romantic universe from above, from the perspective of Spenser's Nature, Shakespeare has avoided an abstract discussion of his philosophical point of view. His metaphysics are translated into terms of human sensibilities. The transformation of Hermione's statue is the human shape of Shakespearean revelation.

BIBLIOGRAPHY

NOTES

BIBLIOGRAPHY

Bacon, Francis. *The Advancement of Learning*, selections in *Seventeenth-Century Prose and Poetry*, ed. Frank Warnke and Alexander Witherspoon, 2nd ed. New York, 1963.

Bentley, Gerald. "Shakespeare and the Blackfriars Theatre." *Shakespeare Survey*, I (1948), 38–50.

Bethell, S. L. *The Winter's Tale: A Study*. London, 1947.

Browne, Sir Thomas. *The Works of Sir Thomas Browne*, ed. Geoffrey Keynes, vol. I. London, 1928.

Bryant, Jerry H. "*The Winter's Tale* and the Pastoral Tradition." *Shakespeare Quarterly*, XIV (1963), 387–398.

Bush, Douglas. *Prefaces to Renaissance Literature*. Cambridge, Mass., 1965.

——— "Two Roads to Truth: Science and Religion in the Early Seventeenth Century." *ELH*, VIII (1941).

Castiglione, Baldassare. *The Book of the Courtier*, trans. Sir Thomas Hoby. London (Everyman), 1928.

Coghill, Nevill. "Six Points of Stage-Craft in *The Winter's Tale*." *Shakespeare Survey*, XI (1958), 31–41.

Frye, Northrop. "Nature and Nothing," in *Essays in Shakespearean Criticism*, ed. Gerald Chapman. Princeton, 1965.

——— "Recognition in *The Winter's Tale*," in *Fables of Identity*. New York, 1963.

Greene, Robert. *The Second Part of Conny-Catching . . .* , ed. G. B. Harrison. Bodley Head Quartos, London, 1923.

41

Honigmann, E. A. "Secondary Sources of *The Winter's Tale*." *Philological Quarterly*, XXXIV (1955), 27–38.

Hooker, Richard. *The Laws of Ecclesiastical Polity*, vol. I. London (Everyman), 1907.

Kermode, Frank, ed. *The Tempest* by William Shakespeare, 6th ed. London, 1957.

Knight, G. Wilson. *The Crown of Life*. London, 1948.

Knights, L. C. "Shakespeare's Sonnets," in *Explorations*. New York, 1947.

—— "King Lear," in *Some Shakespearean Themes*. London, 1964.

Lawlor, John. "*Pandosto* and the Nature of Dramatic Romance." *Philological Quarterly*, XLI (1962), 96–113.

Lewis, C. S. *The Allegory of Love*. London, 1936.

Long, John. *Shakespeare's Use of Music: The Final Comedies*. Gainesville, Fla., 1963.

Milton, John. *The Poems of John Milton*, ed. Helen Darbishire. Oxford Standard Authors, London, 1958.

—— *Prose Writings*, ed. K. M. Burton. London (Everyman), 1958.

Pafford, J. H. P., ed. *The Winter's Tale* by William Shakespeare. London, 1963.

Panofsky, Erwin. *Studies in Iconology*. New York, 1962.

Puttenham, George (?). *The Arte of English Poesie*, in *Elizabethan Critical Essays*, ed. G. Gregory Smith, vol. II. London, 1904.

Sidney, Sir Philip. *An Apology for Poetry*, in *Elizabethan Critical Essays*, ed. G. Gregory Smith, vol I. London, 1904.

—— *The Prose Works of Sir Philip Sidney*, ed. Albert Feuillerat, vols. I and II. London, 1962.

Spenser, Edmund. *The Poems of Spenser,* ed. J. C. Smith
and E. De Selincourt. Oxford Standard Authors, London,
1912.

Spivack, Bernard. *Shakespeare and the Allegory of Evil.* New
York, 1958.

Tayler, Edward William. *Nature and Art in Renaissance Literature.* New York and London, 1964.

Whitaker, Virgil K. *Shakespeare's Use of Learning.* San Marino,
Calif., 1953.

Wolff, Samuel Lee. *The Greek Romances and Elizabethan
Prose Fiction.* New York, 1912.

Woodhouse, A. S. P. "Nature and Grace in The Faerie Queene."
ELH, XVI (1949).

NOTES

1. Sir Philip Sidney, *An Apology for Poetry,* in *Elizabethan Critical Essays,* ed. G. Gregory Smith (London, 1904), I, 170.

2. Frank Kermode, ed., *The Tempest* by William Shakespeare (London, 1957), p. liv.

3. *The Faerie Queen,* in *The Poems of Spenser,* ed. J. C. Smith and E. De Selincourt (London, 1912); all Spenser references are to the 1965 reprint of this edition in the Oxford Standard Authors series.

4. Douglas Bush, *Prefaces to Renaissance Literature* (Cambridge, Mass., 1965), pp. 49–51, gives a brief summary of Renaissance conceptions of hierarchic values.

5. See Erwin Panofsky, "Father Time," in *Studies in Iconology* (New York, 1962), for Time as devourer; also the *Rape of Lucrece* catalogues images of Time, ll. 925ff.

6. L. C. Knights, "Shakespeare's Sonnets," in *Explorations* (New York, 1947), p. 78.

7. S. L. Bethell, *The Winter's Tale: A Study* (London, 1947), pp. 36–44, lists the various blendings of Christian and pagan references. My point is not to neglect the subtle mixture of such references in the play but only to generalize about the values that the characters act upon— Apollo is the one powerful divinity mentioned. As will be seen, I disagree with Bethell's conclusions about "timelessness."

8. John Long, *Shakespeare's Use of Music: The Final Comedies* (Gainesville, Fla., 1963), pp. 25–33.

9. Jerry H. Bryant, "*The Winter's Tale* and Pastoral Tradition," *Shakespeare Quarterly,* XIV (1963), 390.

10. Long, pp. 68–70.

11. Gerald Bentley, "Shakespeare and the Blackfriars Theatre," *Shakespeare Survey,* I (1948), esp. 48.

12. E. A. Honigmann, "Secondary Sources of *The Winter's Tale,*" *Philological Quarterly,* XXXIV (1955), 27–30.

13. Bethell, p. 64.

14. Nevill Coghill, "Six Points of Stage-Craft in *The Winter's Tale*," *Shakespeare Survey*, XI (1958), 34–35.

15. J. H. P. Pafford, ed., *The Winter's Tale* by William Shakespeare (London, 1963), p. 69, note.

16. G. Wilson Knight, *The Crown of Life* (London, 1948), p. 98.

17. All citations are to the Pafford text and will be given in parentheses.

18. John Milton, "Of Education," in *Prose Writings*, ed. K. M. Burton (London, 1958), p. 320.

19. Baldassare Castiglione, *The Book of the Courtier*, trans. Sir Thomas Hoby (London, 1928), p. 268.

20. Northrop Frye, "Nature and Nothing," in *Essays in Shakespearean Criticism*, ed. Gerald Chapman, p. 40.

21. See C. S. Lewis, *The Allegory of Love* (London, 1936), pp. 324–326, for the differences between the Garden of Adonis and the Bower of Bliss.

22. Cf. *Paradise Lost*, in *The Poems of John Milton*, ed. Helen Darbishire, pp. 207–208, esp. the punning of "savour," "sapience."

23. Francis Bacon, *The Advancement of Learning*, in *Seventeenth-Century Prose and Poetry*, ed. Frank Warnke and Alexander Witherspoon (New York, 1963), p. 53.

24. Northrop Frye, "Recognition in *The Winter's Tale*," in *Fables of Identity* (New York, 1963), p. 115.

25. See A. S. P. Woodhouse, "Nature and Grace in *The Faerie Queene*," *ELH*, XVI (1949), for a fourfold distinction in senses of "grace" which I follow. Bethell notes (pp. 38–39) the way the term is casually introduced in talk with Polixenes (I. ii. 95–97); I do not agree that it is necessarily a pun on the Christian sense of "grace." The secular sense that Woodhouse sees in *The Faerie Queene* could apply; I use "grace" in the sense of providential intervention in the natural realm as the highest sense of grace in *The Winter's Tale*—see Woodhouse, p. 207, sense (ii) of "grace."

26. Castiglione, p. 32.

27. Richard Hooker, *The Laws of Ecclesiastical Polity* (London, 1907), I, 186.

28. See Bethell, pp. 60–61, on Leontes comic loss of control in his madness.

29. See Puttenham, *The Arte of English Poesie*, in *Elizabethan*

Critical Essays, ed. G. Gregory Smith, II, 187–189, for an indication of the breadth of meaning "art" had; Puttenham speaks of art as "coadiutor," "mender," "imitator," and "contrary" of nature. See Edward Tayler, *Nature and Art in Renaissance Literature* (New York and London, 1964), p. 26, for discussion of the philosophical scope of the terms "nature" and "art"—together the terms enable man to classify all his moral perceptions.

30. Samuel Lee Wolff, *The Greek Romances and Elizabethan Prose Fiction* (New York, 1912), p. 381.

31. John Lawlor, "*Pandosto* and the Nature of Dramatic Romance," *Philological Quarterly,* XLI (1962), 99–100; the essay as a whole makes little reference to Shakespeare's use of time but discusses differences between the 1588 romance and the 1610–11 play in terms of characterization.

32. Wolff, p. 7; small sections of Xenophon had been translated but Chariton and others were not rendered until the eighteenth century.

33. Frye uses the term "diptych," esp. in "Recognition in *The Winter's Tale,*" p. 107.

34. Bernard Spivack, *Shakespeare and the Allegory of Evil* (New York, 1958), pp. 310–311, briefly mentions this resemblance; Pafford discusses the abstract quality of the chorus: "It is only natural that *Time* should arrogate to himself power to which he is proverbially entitled . . . It is quite another matter to say that author or audience subscribe to this" (p. 168).

35. Hooker, I, 177.

36. See Musidorus' mild rebuke of Pyrocles for excessive praise of the Arcadian landscape; the outburst of eloquence is dissociated from the actuality of the scene. Sir Philip Sidney, *The Prose Works of Sir Philip Sidney,* ed. Albert Feuillerat, I, 57–58. Pafford (p. 97, note) mentions that a possible "source" for Florizel's speech on Perdita's "acts," (IV. iv. 135–146), is Sidney's *Prose Works,* II, 53–54.

37. Subsequent quotations from Act IV, scene iv, are identified by line number only; full references are given for quotations from other scenes.

38. Several layers of irony are usually extracted from the exchange —the fact, for example, that Polixenes and Perdita intend to do just the opposite of what they say concerning marrying the gentle scion to a wild stock. Tayler (pp. 136–137) speaks of Perdita being revealed in

a later scene as a queen by nature whereas she appears in the festival to be a queen only by the art of disguise. I have preferred not to linger on "ironies" simply because they are usually secondary to the immediate impact of the greater part of the scene.

39. See *The Poems of John Milton,* pp. 450–451, ll. 132–152. Of course, the "Lycidas" pastoral is conceived explicitly in terms of the poet's trade and refers primarily to literary tradition.

40. See Woodhouse, pp. 217–218, on the extent to which the ideal of chastity can be grounded in nature.

41. Robert Greene, *The Second Part of Conny-Catching,* ed. G. B. Harrison (London, 1923), pp. 30–35. Table of contents lists the technical terms.

42. Sir Thomas Browne, *The Works of Sir Thomas Browne,* ed. G. Keynes (London, 1928), I, 22–23.

43. Sidney, *Prose Works,* I, 18.

44. Tayler, p. 140.

45. Castiglione, p. 32.